THE SOLITARY

In memory of my father, Murray Carlin.

THE SOLITARY
VUYELWA CARLIN

seren

Seren is the book imprint of
Poetry Wales Press Ltd.
57 Nolton Street, Bridgend, Wales, CF31 3AE
www.seren-books.com

ISBN 978-1-85411-470-9

A CIP record for this title is available from the British Library.

The publisher acknowledges the financial assistance of the Welsh Books Council.

Cover painting: 'Angel Rising from Genoa' by Lorraine Bewsey.
Oil and gold leaf on board. www.lorrainesartstudio.co.uk

Printed in Bembo by Bell and Bain, Glasgow

Contents

MAGDALENA, LECH, JOSEPH

Magdalena at Three Months

1.
Thirty minutes old, imago –
slicked hair, dark eyes of no-colour –
alert gazer, unamazed, knowing nothing: Little Thumb

in translucence, all set: what lies
in the mind's most ancient lands, the first-made,
before sense, and thought?

2.
Three months, eyes still smoke-colour –
bluish, we think – little burnished world-mirrors;
here are squares of light, tree-shapes,

and here we are. I took you outside;
we gazed back, into the house –

your mother's face, there in the far, far dim
was too much for you: such grief!

3.
We posed you at the foot of the blasted tree –
new, on old charredness:

then against the valley, on a high meadow;
was it the hugeness of air you loved,
the sedate-striding masses of it, a paced breeze?

4.
You have such strength of mind,
such deep-grooved palms: hardly possible
you don't talk.

But you are still breaking your nerve-path;
your long, thin, adult fingers stray –
aim, strayingly; puzzles of dust.

5.
Interspersed: your landscape, its clarities,
and here and there, a shade of rock, or tree,
seen without eyes –

shadows of givens,
concealed paths, green threads through the forest.

Magdalena at Six Months

1.
Mid-throw, on top of the air-arch, you hover,
hang collected, like Nijinsky,
just doing the next thing. You know more –

have an inkling of this matter, that:
you can search – for a while –

but stuff sits lightly, still –
rolls, after a bit, quietly into the dark.

2.
You might laugh, now, at a blown-away hat.

And the shadow of your futures,
that great hanging parkland, with its groves,
all those paths – ghosts yet –

has passed off-centre
– or we have turned away charmed, charm-distracted.

3.
Songs sung before birth
no longer send you into quietness:
they have dropped down into the dark –
blind slivers, pressed wisps, on the ocean floor.

4.
You are built, build –
what is made up, and what copied down?
what is caught, what alights?

You have known, already, dreams; some bad;
your new sorrows stir old constructs –
arc into future-shock:

you are becoming loose in Time, like all of us –
clinging, swinging on its vast lianas!

5.
A daffodil, a dandelion – something sturdy,
no-nonsense; you have your reasons! –

and you air-walk,
stay, air-held – as far as you know –
a catcher, a fisher, a drawing density, fierce almost.

Magdalena at One Year

1.

You have a good line in bitterest weeping
– small things – what loss,
what griefs, wailing in death-corridors?

– Spin the fish, the little heavy fish,
the bright, primitive clays,
and you are happy: – uncle-art,

and he fascinates you, with his unsmiling eyes
– on a lonely road,

immune to you – *Go away baby.*
Unsnubbed, you study him.

2.

Your laugh distilled water; quaverless:

the earths separate:
you see your ending – know yourself, almost,
in a mirror –

joy of self! this; this lump:
that, other, you finger, scratchingly.

3.

And you are setting, settling
into your new, buzzing matter – everlasting,
pinned into the universe; pinning –

soils, waters, airs,
changed for ever; all this vast thin stardust
rejigged, a little, for ever:

and the moveless past
scanned, picked over

by the little sticky feet, or feelers,
of that atom-cluster twenty-one months back.

Magdalena at Two Years

1.

One could draw you now,
press out a clay likeness; the baby bone-knolls,
dells, are hardening, slightly,

into old Slavness
– barely – the delicacy of it! –
(and the other traces, flakelets,

transparencies of deposits? –
of North Country, apple-cheeked in the daguerrotype,

the red-dusty Dutch trekkers,
the half-legendary Spanish Doña?)

2.

You talk, and talk; sing and sing –
Ride a Cock Horse to Banbury Cross,

See a fine lady upon a white horse,
Rings on her toes wherever she goes.

3.

You watch him, uncle, Mr. Solitary,
writing his careful diary: lean on his knee.
He accepts you – just –

half-tame, nerves held in:
you are quiet, a porcelain girl
– anyone else, and the pencil would be yours –
in the emperor's china palace,

amid his chinking, fragile flowers:
intent, understanding without knowing –

his thin-walled city,
the winds wild at the gates.

4.
Death has touched you, and not touched you –
Dziadek spi.*
You watched, calm, earth to frozen earth.

5.
English – to the half-attending ear – twitters like birds:
Polish is scrunched snow, ice-creak:
each strange to the other –
each, to you, everyday, workaday, common-or-garden.

6.
You are ill, too often –
odd viruses.

We know of the ancient sea;
ur-swimmers, beaten out beneath thought;

is your clutch of cells, not yet quite dry,
jarred, by the dredged handfuls

– raw heads and bloody bones –
hauled up by the dream-messengers, dream-divers?

* *Granddad is sleeping*

Magdalena at Three Years

Reality...
there's no station
on our journey's route
where it won't be waiting.
  – ('Reality' by Wislawa Szymborska)

1.
Disillusion: de-goddessed,
you hurl, whirl, roar,
tilt at the boulders – unsized, strewn

to the edge of things. (The sanctuary
where they lie, the vast overarching quiet,
bird-trailed, you don't see –

just this stone, this –
scored with what unreadables?)

2.
And that uncle, stranger
walking his crooked mile
– how should you know? –
he's learned to suffer you, pressing at his knee:

but one day, dragged raw
on the world's sharp armature,
he sent a dark look –

eye to eye, batting home.
– Aloneness, wind howling through the stones,
you wept, and wept.

Magdalena at Three-and-a-Half Years

1.
A smile – a dazzler –
as you close the door gently:
soft chinkings, and later in the dim passage

you glint, hung about
with heirloom necklaces; amber, the square jades,
the delicate string of shells,
sixty years old.

2.
We are busy: you wear solitude
easily as the Oxfam satin
– your princess-dress: play, and play

– singing snatches of song,
little pieces of your life, sung –
with the buttons, marbles, coins.
You sort, stash.

You place the scattered cards carefully back,
one by one, into the box,
unhasting:
beat of the grass-threader, mud-plaiter.

3.
Great drifts of tellings:
words wheel and spin –
whorls of words seen vaguely;

and doubletons, charmed, indivisible –
wiggly worm, buzzing bee.

Stories are laid down,
pressed in, before Reason –
the slipper's fit, the bales of spite-spun gold,
the sleep like Death in the dark forest.

– So we yearn over the Pearl, lost and gone,
the black mere,
the muttered snowbound sleep of Gawain.

Lech at Four Months

1.

Contemplator, lacking terrors
– young Gabriel Oak,
stepping firm through the mud, stoic in dust

(your Polish farmer-uncle with his dusty hair,
that tiny village, staring):

no wolvish Spartan hillside for you
– not likely!
– fine boy, you'd have sent the old king,

rotting, madding with mortality,
into fits of joy.

2.

Magdalena's eyes are leaf-brown, old bracken,
backed with gold –
forest-water late-sunned.

Yours are dark, blackbrown, shine darkly
like oil – the richness of it
running down upon the beard,
*upon the beard of Aaron...**

– you are dew of Hermon.
And you sit, balanced,
in the warm waters of the babies' pool,

solemnly thrilled,
a good staunch working cherub.

* *From Psalm 133*

Three Poems for Joseph, Turned 30

1. Cut of Bone

Boneset: the skeleton you'll die with,
unevenness of jaw that only I see:
– all those bones!

caves, valleys, of bones:
bone-story – skull, femur, phalange –
prints in rock, letters in stone,

scrutinized – and a light breaks over:
– what's told?
The armature of you (minutely skewed) –

in ten thousand years' time, a young man, tall,
with exceptional teeth:
not written in bone is your strangerhood –

other-wired, grappling
with endless, fitful plays –
the litheness behind the eyes,

swoops, ripples – the weather of the face,
soul-shadows. For you (for all of you)
it's numbers, form; the markered march

of days, years (*That was May the 4th, and I was twenty*)
– comfort of line, the immutable.
In the valley of bones,

you lie – large brain-cavity –
wrenched, probably,
away from the solid trigs, the long

long elegancies of rule.

2. Chaste Planes

Severe planes of face:
chaste as maths, as stone: – *No,*
to the tenner, offered – *I've got money.*

– Savants, oddballs: you suffer the fierce sun
of this blinding garden – Babel
of mores, of the unspoken: souls

beating about your heads. Exquisite systems,
tipping – constantly – out of true;
your home is the distilled deeps

– matter rendered down to mind –
where beautiful equations might be found,
where the arrow of time

is double-headed: not strange, not to you.
– Cast up, iridescences fading,
I want to rewind time, you'd say.

3. Bird of Paradise Flower

– The Cape, mountains leaning in,
sheared off, drawn sharp: the ash of your grandfather

strewn over the hilly vineyard: you liked him
well enough, in your way – his soul's light shaken, estranged,
through your prisms. *Murray's dead,* you said,

Mustn't laugh. People slide by; you're disengaged
from the mad fool of heart:
kindliness of geometries, consolation of the just poise,

elegant proof: – once, as you flew home eastward,
time bounded ahead, righted itself –
you saw the sun rise at midnight

and were joyful. In the Kirstenbosch gardens
(cool, trembling patterns of winter light)
we played *What flower are you?* – Metaphor,

that interloper, lurching out of the deep like Jaws,
and your nerves plucked to bleeding – *Don't know, don't know.*

You are the Bird of Paradise flower, no other:
precision-petalled, a piked beauty – finicky dweller,

singular. *Murray goodbye for ever* –
words like stones, chinking as you set them out,
gamely, astray on the stony desert, the unreverberating plain.

PLAQUES AND TANGLES

Seals in the Dry Valley

In the Arctic South, but snowless –
the blown valley,
everlasting charge of wind-cavalry;

black blades of rock,
wind-whetted: it is dry as Mars.
The thousand-year dead inhabit it –

ancients of days rock-perched.
The wind roars through eyeholes,
has scoured them out –

gourds of bone, of wind:
spices of wind,
and the packed pulps, brain-lumps,

tossed into that inverted bowl –
density of old stardust, moving and shaking;
grass-meal, somewhere,

or up-spiralled, nudging at gravity's blue rim.
Odd atoms, no-mass,
existing and not-existing –

are they making forever to the edge of things?
– And iron on iron,
dog-heads poised,

you valley carapaces
keen: eyelash-spikes in the wind,
ivories, whittled slowly, slowly, over wind-centuries.

Dead Child with a Bible

A Victorian photograph

This is not you: stopped flesh, an It.
Bloodless, the little bowl of skull,
its hanging of face –

the unswirled purple
slides down through unresisting valves –
the upper veins are empty.

You – It – was eased into a Sunday suit,
propped on that parlour chair,
finger-bones curved into a bookrack –

later, they'll be snapped flat.
– Eyes, unstaring under pushed-up lids:
not like jet, or black agates –

stones have a presence, play with light;
not like anything – the windowless dead,
unportrayable.

You: irradiation of the body,
snap and flash of nerve, thought-maker:
your first cells seethed with you.

You pummelled your time like clay! –
beat out a new universe,
changed everything for ever.

– There's no where of you, now:
yet you roar in the firmament,
stretch, twist, wrench the strands of us still.

That Face, is it Yours Still?

(in memory of Ken)

Ten years – and the mystery of it,
the yearning delight of elegy! –
...the peace of my years
in the long green grass... *We cling

to the emptied flesh: juiceless skin still holding
over tendon-web; blood-grains
in runnels of arterial dust; wisps of nerve
– sere crisps of hardly-anything.

Process of matter, passionless –
taking its time, thinking of nothing –
and the lithe, binding soul? held, somehow,
out of timespace, but drifting between atoms?

– But is that face yours yet?
(*I'm pacified – a little* – said Heathcliff.)
Flesh fascinates – your particles alter,
creep through the earth – ride the universe –

collide with the saints, Hitler, and all of us.
Once met, there's no true parting, ever.
His electrons cling to ours –
the man in the garden, the changed/unchanged tissue of him.

* *Leo Marks*

27

The Incredible Shrinking Man
Walks on the Common

Slant of late ray, October; angled acutely,
dragged, thickened with air:

look front-on, at the light-path –
and the gossamers show up, sheer,

tacking blade to blade, the whole hillside gauzy.
Shift the eyes, they're gone – just the warp
of the old rough grass. Bend down,

examine: nothing. Touch? – the fingertip's a steel hull.
– The shrinking man picks his way

over harsh clods, beneath the net
of glinting ropes, in the diffused light:
one day he'll whirl with atoms,

massless, bend time. He touches the flattish trunks,
soaring leafless: leans an ear, hears the swish

in hidden pipes. Where's God?
The dust-speck of his heart yearns out unmet.

– The anchoress, pulsed through with sorrow and light:
All manner of things... – every pattern of cell?
every skew, drift? –

...shall be well – God's cracked feet, dipped
in the runnels of cool chlorophyll? This dot of man, priceless,
dashing his terrors against Christ?

The Pool of Bethzatha

...He said to him, "Do you want to be healed?" – John 5:6

At least, battening, they understood each other,
forty years' pain and he – his pillar, spine-
hollowed slightly: he would watch alone
for God's rare breath – if it was so – wave-feather,

the minders' rush, the first twig-armed bather.
The riffled water's fearful lap and groan! –
and beyond, the wind, the grass-smell, goaty green –
his dreams lately, in stiff sinew-tether?

Austerity of wholeness, the wild air!
He had chosen runnels of stone, wormcasts:
now he must tilt on paths, ribbons of gusts,

cold with unlagging, the old pain ripped out.
He walks, still wobbly, through brilliant dust-whirr;
the endless sanctuary, chisels of light.

Guy Fawkes and the Torturers

A cobweb-scrawl – he could barely hold the pen;
he signed – just – a bag of loose joints for the flames.
He was racked for days, in the forbidden rooms,*
the cellars of the dark soul, fallen.

One day, hour, minute more – to the God of pain
he clings; wrenches to mind the vales and loams,
beloved, where they crouch, the lodged names
– gouged at last from the deep bed, scraped from bone.

The fracturing sticks of this incarnation,
its twisting strings: the torture-scholars grind
the rope and tackle: crush the shadow, blind

and dumb; they'd pincer out the nerves of God
if they only could – pay back the terrible Word,
the act, intolerable, of creation.

* *Although it was regularly used, torture was, in fact, illegal.*

The 2nd Razumovsky Quartet*
and the Reductionists

for the Solaris String Quartet

The tragic question is thrown, over and over:
the stiffening delicate bones, the piano-strings curled,
broken; he was almost done with the world,
maddened – the pipe and rustle in the perfect ear!

Then a kind of peace – the comet, moveless mover
in the early morning, long, long-tailed:
a hundred million miles, icicled,
a mud-ball trail; a startling pearl, caller.

Stuff-bundles, blind, do we burrow through time,
intent on breath, the split of cell, graceless?
Is tragedy a tossed-off, chancy spark?

Stone-ears, at the feet of genius
he threw despair: the music pressed through dark,
the frozen runnels, to deep mind's deep game.

* *Beethoven, Op. 59, No. 2*

Plaques and Tangles

(for Mary Forrest)

Portions of...grey matter...become steadily clouded with two separate forms of cellular debris: clumpy brown spherical **plaques** *floating between the neurons, and long black stringy* **tangles** *choking neurons from inside their cell membranes...tens of millions of synapses dissolve away.*
　　　　　　　　　　　　– (*From* The Forgetting: Understanding Alzheimer's:
　　　　　　　　　　　　　A Biography of a Disease *by David Shenk*)

1. Ellen
born 1908

What's your name? you ask, over and over:
but answers slip off, unlodging.
– Oh, the tiny, stiffening ear-bones quiver still,

grasp at sounds, spin, mould – a word's thrown;
and our names all throng the placeless past –
row upon row, unfired.

Your own name clings about you – *I'm Ellen.*
Bundle of sticks, a marionette unstrung,
you slump, slide –

you haven't walked in years.
– But pace (as it were) the same little, bleak shore,
strip walled off with fog, the sea vague beyond.

A long way to Pen-y-coedcae,
a long way home. You read (blind)
from the anciently furrowed rocks – sought by poets –

beneath the blasted forest,
its matted deadwood: declaim – softly, almost singsong –
Wanderer, your exile.

2. Lydia
born 1915

Tiny Lydia, each little bone outlined;
translucent Lydia – the vein-map of you:

your fragile fierce arm clings –
Help me – I've been wrong all my life.

Miniature ivory, flake of alabaster,
airy puff of hair; you mark at a touch –

fairyish thing bruised by the pea
twenty mattresses down. *I'm wrong –*

he said so – and you know it – over and over;
Thumbelina's seed of heart, pinched with cold.

Brittle, pressed blanchflower, you hold on –
the lodged hook drags, and drags.

3. Maisie
1920–2005

I am like a pelican of the wilderness: I am like an owl of the desert.
　　　　　　　　　　　　　　　　　　　　　– Psalm 102

1.
You perch on some stack – lost –
gaze round this habitation, its arcane forms,
these incognitos: your face old cloth –

specked, easily torn; but your blue eyes (puzzled)
much as they were: *Where am I? What is this place?*

Tendrils of nerve fizzle out –
you touched your rough chin, cried out horrified –
But I'm old! How can I be old?

2.
You've forgotten the dear name, your father's –
but hold to him: *Is my father still living?* –
I thought not… oh yes, I loved my father.

(Your mother's fading; she threatened, locked you up
– *To tell the truth,*
we were thankful when she died.)

You remember the weekend walks,
how he never scolded; your travels, and the Greek sun.

You've forgotten – at last – his long decline;
how you'd leave food for him, ready on the table,
return from work, find him gone – *And I'd go searching…*

3.
A visit once, from that man-friend we'd heard of
(*He bled her dry*): he was black-browed still, a Don –
held your hand, gazed meaningfully. Who was he? –

you'd no idea – yet knew him,
had found him again, in some deep, watered place –
you smiled, and smiled. When he went,

that reappearance dropped away at once –
uncatchable, the thread of now
(knots of dried-up finger-joints, the needle's fine eye).

4.
– Happenings stir the air, reshape everything:
the past's here-there –
death-mask of incalculable perfection,

cut with delicatest lines –
the demi-thoughts, winging by; the gone dreams; all the
                                                    forgettings.

4. Gwen
born 1919

1.
You tip tea, gently, over the table –
tranquilly watch, as it runs and spreads,
slows, stills;

or you drop food on the floor, intently:
– *But why not?* you say.

Fascination of substances (it seems),
of playing with stuffs
– the two-year-old, squeezing butter –

and your eyes are as guiltless, as unknowing.
– But that firm freshness,
that buzzing, gulping bloominess!

– not you – your forest of mind
(those uphurrying, bendy little trees)

is drying, dying.

2.
Its stiffened groves are rung through – from time to time –
with Pan's terrible shout:
– *Who are those people? Look, them there –*
stay with me, stay with me.

But the fear's brief, fades off somewhere.

3.
With wide, mild eyes,
you'll punch – suddenly, hard and without spite:

arm-jerk, bypassing the pale husks
– delicate shed shells of etiquette –
a courier, blocked-off,
pushing through by an older, wilder, obscurer path.

4.
Oftener now, you speak Gwennish –
a jabber of tongues, clear – I believe – to you:

untranslatable as dream-coinages,
that elvish gold tumbling out as charcoal into the light.

5.
Six months back, you puzzled:
where on earth were you?
Give me some names – I'll see what rings a bell –

That's gone – caught in hanks of clotted threads –
the keen, keen, tender filaments that once waved, tossed,
                                        irradiated.

5. Hatty
1906-2003

1.
Bag of twigs,
you'd glower over stained silks
– had just poured puree over yourself –,

dare us – a tiny iron fist poised,
to approach with our cloths: none ventured.

You were the Red Queen:
you were Fury.

2.
Your grandmotherly days: pink-cheeked,
mouth primmed humorously,
you stood by a uniformed boy, on the bureau.

You'd shrunk and shrunk –
pared down to brittle, flailing bones and wild hair.

The soft moss gouged away,
you were all sharp flints –
an imp, a changeling.

3.
Now and then, some nerve-storm would be stayed,
some gadfly of the brain, sleep:

you'd submit to washing, a few quick hairclips,
and in a voice soft and low,
would murmur thanks. – Then you'd surge back,

raging: rattling with loose rings,
you'd pinch;
kick with de-slippered, paper-thin feet.

4.
Time to die: for two weeks
you ate nothing, drank nothing.

Dead, you were a bluish wisp –
malleable, miniature arms in lacy sleeves:

at last, we could fasten the fiddly pearl buttons,
brush out, dispose, your gorgeous, heavy, slaty hair.

6. Dorothy
born 1922

1.
You've been knocked for six – suddenly –
your blood is gorging on itself,
gulps iron, sickens with metal: you lie snow-white.

2.
Long ago, black-sleeved
(your Rose Red days – untouched deep-blooded lips and ebony hair),
you swirled the cloth out from the great bolts,

snapped its eddyings dead-straight
(but wayward silk you stilled with precise gentle palm)
– wielded unswerving shears.

3.
Two years you've roamed these corridors:
where is Mr. Warren (of Warren Bros)?
You search your empty handbag – there's a ticket somewhere.

The past's fugitive jostlings, the jutting present:
you're looked-for – *Do you want me now, Madam? Here I am* –
must move – you're blocking the doorway.

4.
Quieted, now: perhaps they're gone,
those paths, a maze of them, each blocked off
– impassable deadtangle. Was it like those half-dreams,

outcropping into the cored Now? –
a dozen bundles on the head of a pin:
some loss; a skewed, almost-joyful finding; then loss again.

7. Rosalie
born 1918

1.
You are Patience:
you speak no word, not now.

The girl on the dresser, with her fair ringlets,
looks away, as you do still –
but catch, hold your harebell eyes,

you'll smile – always:
when happy, dancingly, as if speech hovered near;
politely, obediently, if you're sad, or ill.

2.
You were walking, a few weeks ago –
held on either side, you'd pad with small steps,
unobjecting.

Softly, mutely, you dropped down a rung or two:
lingered very gently when we stood you up;
sitting, you hung your head.

A grey shadow sat on your face,
your smiles were late, and hesitant.

3.
You're in bed to stay:
you've lightened, and brightened – still, perhaps,
have some way to go.

Yet the shade's still there – lightest of veils.
Meek lamb, you've let it be known

that you are turning, very quietly,
back to earth.

8. Tudor
1908–2004

1.
– For weeks now, silence:
you are stiff as a board, your body smooth,
white – as alabaster, as frozen Little Kay:

distilled water, unflawed crystal, slab of Carrara –
the long innocence of you
a pearliness visible.

The Reverend Tudor Jones,
your valley church: I imagine its flags' chill,
the soft misty rain: you, stone of the corner, plain-cut.

2.
When you could still speak –
rags of memories, or sometimes the Lord's Prayer,
deeply etched, rolling out whole –

you said suddenly, *God,*
why won't you come for me? how long must I wait?
– a blade of light,

a sharp clear swish,
a ripple, one last time,
through the clogged, petrifying stalks.

3.
Death taps, at last – firmly, this time –
offers an arm, warm,
out of this troublous place,

this room of vague shapes; this tangle of you.
 – Yet your eyes gleam;
thought-stripped,

loosening, you're hard by
the vast spaces. – See, see, where you, and Christ, stream
through nerve-clinker; the firmament.*

* cf Marlowe's *Dr. Faustus*

MURRAY
MY FATHER, 1921-2004

Footless Bird, Cape Town, July 2004

Cool Southern winter – sunny, cloudless,
and an under-chill:
the outdoor café on the waterfront (open all year)
is its feeding-ground;

little neat stilts of equal length
– did it hatch so?
Did someone catch it, snip off its birdfeet?

Balancer, clown-bird –
its wings whir, veer into swirl, counter-swirl –
language of air beyond delicateness.

Perchless, ever-moving, it eats, eats –
stalks near shoes, even on tables:
charmer (it seems); the botched, buttering us up –
Freddy the Human Frog, bounding and smiling,

offering a calloused hand.
– Thirty years ago, hereabouts, a group marched by singing,
with a placard – *The Friendship Club* – and a bag of tangerines:
you, recently dead, told me of it.

The air shines; so close, these mountains,
pressing at the city's edge!
You're ash, gritty, scattered in the vineyard.

Tumblers at the water's edge –
one somersaults through flaming hoops, and suchlike;
one leaps about, does the patter.

We're rooted. – When you were a child,
the farmhands gave their Christmas entertainment
(*A kind of revenge it was,* you said) – they danced and danced,
all evening, and into the hot, hot night;

you, your small indomitable mother (who could face down a bull),
watchful on the veranda,
as they stamped and pounded and sang and pounded and stamped.

Cape Point, July 2004

Two seas –
the chilly, fierce Atlantic,
the warm Indian: even at fifty-five

I'd imagined clashing lines,
a jagged seam of waters; coldwater claws
digging into blue buoyancies.

(Northerly, it beats grey-white,
the Atlantic, against the Hebrides:
feet aching, icy, in the waters of Harris –

its black-rock caverns smelling of sea –
its oysters, essence of sea –
pellets of sea slipping over the throat).

Africa – calling – baked dry:
hill after hill of vivid brush, huge mad medleys of succulents:
no crops – *It's too dry; too dry.*

But inland from the Cape, some pineapple-fields,
needing little water: soused lumps
– soaked through like slabs aeons beneath the water-table –

impossible as the silly frail wings of bumblebees
or daffodils gleaming through frost-press:
– *Magic*, you'd say. An hour before death,

you perked up, had tea; heart cracking (at last)
with the unspoken; the clearcut mountain
lying against the window.

Constantia Chapel, Cape Town, July 2004

Knot of tie – no long death-robe, or Jesus-frock
(where he gambols with lambs,
pastel-eyed, Goldilocks – who called

the sinewy wind-hardened fishermen, walked on sea
with tough, cold-cracked feet): framed in pine,
you looked – momently – asleep. The children peered; ran off.

The quiet grew: smell of fresh wood,
chill gules falling through glass:
vague sounds of play – the boys

among the buttress-roots – common or garden here,
these earth-cleavers; we're the outsiders, the amazed.
– You're lightless: fill the room

with stasis, lack of soul's jolt.
– Strangeness of Lazarus! why, and how?
four days' mudding down of atom;

spiced, swaddled, wept log. – When he emerged, bandages trailing,
shaken through (again) with beat and counter-beat,
arcing thought – what was he? foreshadow of God,

eating fish on the beach? – his smoky hands, nets of galaxies,
holding all the dry bones, the webbing electricities
shot through, for ever, with faint gleams of you.

The Packers, Cape Town, July 2004

Eight boxes in all; a square metre:
a deft job – books, papers, stowed;
box-files of letters, photos – the fair-haired baby, unbreeched,

not a cell in common – yet you: then later, in the strafed Libyan desert
(carried, silently, for sixty years).

Then they wrapped the tarnished silver tea set (heirloom, ugly)
with neat twists, stashed the lumps
fittingly, like drystone-wallers (far little, opulent England!).

Here, the shipment – the vital word,
your skin-flakes (perhaps) in folds of paper:
over there, the charity pile – scraps, impersonals:

The head packer eyed them – *And those?* –
wisp of indication, delicacy of longing – the leather suitcase?

But we must write out the giving, sign it:
scribble with dusty hand,
crouched on cold concrete in the cool, bright sun.

We dug around, hastily, for the other two –
found some suede gloves, and a picture:
then waited, under the azure winter sky of your country –

the sharp wedges of mountain, standing over us;
the little withered drunks, the electrified fences –

and the crazy flora: eight-foot towering cousins
of our pinky roadside mallow;
vast bushes – throwing out wild scent – of our kitchen-sill bay.

Blood in the Clogs, 1945

Evil: the first you knew of the worst was 1946 –
the Winter March over, liberated, flown to Brighton:
How bright, how clean, England seemed –
how rosy-cheeked! – a fresh-painted land,

despite the bombsites. Your friends joined you, soon,
thin as you, but choked with some other thing.
On their march (slow, goaded by panicky guards),
they'd met another, slower: – *They were much thinner – wearing clogs,*

pyjamas. – Pyjamas? – Later, ordered back,
senselessly, in the night, they stumbled over clogs,
fell on slipperiness. The people in pyjamas
lay scattered. In the little unknowing time left,

you pondered it (weighed-upon, already –
those bulldozers, just out of sight).
But it was true puzzlement; you had no inkling – wanted accuracy,
not hindsight; not clever young men saying you'd known.

Rabbi

(*Based on a photograph in the Imperial War Museum.*)

*You have counted up my groaning; put my tears into your bottle;
are they not written in your book?* – Ps.56

They cluster about him shaving his beard, fiddling,
undoing buttons. His eyes – muzzy specks –

hold still, look at death. The men in the camp
put God on trial, found him guilty,
said evening prayers. Bones, ash

of the righteous rise through capillaries, break out of the green,
whizz off – as the charred mash of Hitler,

ground into earth. What waits, at the end of time?
I will take your heart of stone...*
What process, what agony, as the blood seeps in?

They've smashed the tablets of the dead – God's people –
now they swarm; crawl over him
like a tetter. He's set his sights

on us: commands. – God with us,
lungs bursting, turns slowly in the freezing air.

*cf Ezekiel: *And I will remove from your body the heart of stone,
and give you a heart of flesh.*

Kazimierz

(*Old Jewish quarter, Krakow.*)

I am yours, O save me!
For I have sought your commandments. – Ps.119

Handcarts to the ghetto: families pushing, pulling,
waving: a street corner, and an old man

motionless: the wobbly camera stays,
as slowly, seer, he presses trembling fingers to his mouth.
In Isaac's Synagogue the film plays and plays. Wind sighs

along Szeroka and Jakuba Street. Deep shock
is embedded in these old walls. Hans Frank was hanged*

(back with Mother Church, or so he said): but those who stared
on the frenzy? looked at elders stretched gaunt
in the road? – canker, unidentified,

dragging the marrow. – A young man, holy fool,
loving his Poland, shouldering her sins,

roams, rescuing tombstones from pavements, floors;
makes gardens of the dead in the forest –
the birches grown exquisite – quite possibly – from bonemeal,

their trunks alabastrine. A rustly tape
accompanies the film: the cantor sings *Kol Nidre,*
as the black hats bob, and the long coats swing jerkily.

* Frank was Governor-General of occupied Poland, 1939-45.

Remuh Synagogue and Cemetery, Kazimierz

Yet you have crushed us in the haunt of jackals,
and covered us with the shadow of death. – Ps.44

Tiny Remuh, where the remnant sings,
once a month. – They hacked and hacked

at those slabs (the unbearable, steadfast dead) –
then soil, rubbish, more soil, tons of it. Much later,
– everyone dead, or fled – the cemetery was restored; this East wall

– deserted – pieced together with the fragments.
– Not much else to see now, in old Kazimierz – a handful

of inscriptions not quite obliterated,
hard to find: the place was gouged out. – God,

pressed into this net of nerves, grappling:
does he despair of the smiters,
roaring back endlessly, like the sea?

The holy, spread sparse; lightning-cracks of prayer;
the chroniclers, insistent on light: what balance?
– *None,* said Ivan, *Count me out.**

Jacob – that twister – wrestled, would not let go:
all night long, wrenching ball from socket, wrenching out a blessing.

* *Ref.:The Brothers Karamazov*

Ernst Kaltenbrunner

(*Hitler's Security Chief and in charge of the extermination programme; tried at Nuremberg.*)

Look upon your creation, for the earth is full of darkness, full of the haunts of violence. – Ps.74

He dwindled and dwindled, eaten by terror –
his huge head a rawbone. His face was pulled,

by that scar, into a kind of smile.
His brain shut down, he denied everything –
they named him *the man with no signature.*

Click on 'Images' and a shock comes up:
Kaltenbrunner (and the other ten), post-execution. They lie,
ropes trailing, faces turned to camera.

But how peaceful they look! – relieved, emptied out.
They'd spoken of repentance – but mostly had no hope:
they had begun – some of them – to see

what ordinary people saw: some hearts
had developed hairline cracks. Had he, shambling, begun

the trek over the glinting stony desert? the labour
of becoming broken? His lawyer was a fool –

such a fool, he even joked about it – well,
something like a joke:
a drop of cool water, begged of Abraham?

The Hanging of Janusz Pogonowski

(A member of the Polish resistance, Janusz was hanged in Auschwitz, with eleven others, on 19th July 1943, aged 20.)

The floods have lifted up, O Lord, the floods have lifted up their voice; the floods lift up their pounding waves.– Ps.93

Death in the evening: for a moment,
pushed out into the late light,
they thought they'd been freed. – Poland, Poland!

– the Husaria* winging down, lance-silks roaring – :
he kicked the stool over, hanged himself –

choked off the indictment as Hoess* started to read. – Clumps
of faces under the reddish sun: nine hundred Russians

first tried out the gas – *It set my mind at rest...*
said Hoess later; obedient as ever,

he wrote his autobiography in the condemned cell
– passionless, puzzled. He was told to repent –
groped after it, in a way. – The surd of evil:

– squeeze, slew of the heart: the saints cling
– such uncertainty! – run, at times, like the Red Queen:

or they grab chaos – like young Pogonowski –
hurl its dense ball, wreck the show.

★ The Husaria were the Polish 'winged cavalry' of the seventeenth
century, who wore eagle feathers rising above their shoulders.
★ Rudolf Hoess was Commandant of Auschwitz; tried and hanged in 1947.

The Parish Priest and the Malickis, Warsaw, 1943

Lord, how I love your statutes:
they are my meditation all the day long. – Ps.119

Mousy, diligent, they falsified Births and Deaths,
forged certificates of baptism. The priest

(name unknown) was hustled off, in the end,
shot: rubble under the rose madders,
burnt siennas, of the new Old Town,

raised up impeccable after the war. The Malickis
(husband and wife) died too –

arms and legs smashed, saying nothing. – Arc, vault
of evil, leaping the firebreaks (*martyrs' bones...*
said old Brother Balaam): – sludge of a child,

blocking some camp drain; dug in,
stamped down, over and over. – The Desert Fathers,

leathery-dry, pushed on, threshing scrawny crops,
saying the Psalms: pressed against Christ,

his dusty feet, tired eyes. – God, wrecked:
that cry of dereliction, awkward, hooked in time: slow fizz
(sealed in stone) of our complex salvation.

The Stokowskis, Eastern Poland, 1944

(The Stokowski family, Polish peasants, hid Jews during the war.)

My soul waits for the Lord more than watchmen for the morning:
more, I say, than watchmen for the morning. – Ps.130

I remember them as angels,★ said the alien,
the sojourner (heaped with sins, harried). They died for it –

the little house roaring with flame, the family
felled as they ran. Such souls –

cascaded through with light – no choice, they'd say.
– Rotted down, all of them – the Stokowskis,
their neighbours (horrible with fear) – transmuted

to birch-sap: all matter that ever was,
still is. – Christ's atoms
(star-ash, like the rest) seek out the bread and wine;

irradiate. – The holy few, looking past chaos:
...*the apple of God's eye,* said the Stokowskis –

cleared out the tiny cellar by night,
all that summer eked out their miserable food.
– Prayer, that thrown light –: *No cheap grace,* said Bonhoeffer.★

★ Both phrases from *The Righteous* by Martin Gilbert, p.146.
★ Dietrich Bonhoeffer, German Lutheran pastor and opponent of Nazism, was imprisoned by Hitler in 1943 and hanged in 1945.

Hier is kein warum*

(*Auschwitz-Birkenau, visited 2005.*)

Are your wonders known in the darkness,
or your saving help in the land of forgetfulness? – Ps.88

Acres of it: endless grids
of ruined huts: this washblock still stands –

a row of holes, forty or so,
over a cesspit. You were not people – your eyes

were out of bounds – no twines of light,
plays recollected in tranquillity: here's claptrap

– the mouthing saints! – death walking familiarly,
a rag, a bone, a daub (Kazimierz,

its blown empty streets, its vestiges).
– By the emerald ashmeal meadows, granite

of the Memorial: the dark tons, cut plain,
press down on violent shock. – Ash,

raining on the town, never spoken of:
and the terrible, unwieldy dead roll about the land,

unassimilated: plaque upon plaque –
riddled repentance, wrested over and over

from an eluded God: God, waiting
in the ruins, hands full of ash, loam?
                                        ...a mulberry,

lying in the mud, goes one story –
a prisoner found it, gave it, on a leaf, to her friend.

* *There is no 'why' here* (from *If This Is A Man*
  by Primo Levi)

57

THE SOLITARY

The Solitary: Part One

1. Child
A child, a child: the new windows' blank shine,
those navy eyes, those pattern-lacking oils,
unstrung, as yet, together – the white, white balls!
And what is held – what stuff, I mean – in common,

between it, and this I? The tight-packed brain,
birth-furrowed? – and the soul, the seed of the soul:
the rest, all dying, and slough, and constant crawl
of replica: the sprawl ashore, mulch-spin.

A child, I feared colliding of the Earth
with asteroid, stray planet; greenstick,
each day all fresh in fear, lay, in sky-check,

dizzied with spin: and what was God? nightgowned,
he gloomed in space, one arm unmoving forth –
realler were ivory Psyche; Echo, pool-pined.

2.
I read – somewhere – of a man, atheist
as he became; but through his angry days
he sensed – like it or not – the still waters,
the deep drenching beneath the cracked waste.

His mother's Unseen Friend had caught him fast
– that simple God. Ur-wings' delicacies,
precisions in fresh amber, infant clays,
striate the centuries, incise the mist.

And I was graven with the lack of God: –
great starbeat space; the molecule necklace
shuffled together in the lonely seas;

the genius of us, epiphenomenal froth.
Are the prints set? – In that sealed stone, what truth?
slow veer of stirred atoms, recharging blood.

3.
Then – as an older child – with questions
I was buffeted – a blown, rooted thing;
a summer tree, afraid, dense leafage wrung
with wind; against the brutal airs it leans,

resisting willy-nilly, groaning greens,
the great taps creaking – till the winter song
makes easier way through fractals, cat's cradling
of twiggy space. – In the valley of bones

I seemed to be: staring, straining to flesh
this dry heap – what-proclaiming? – these grey drafts.
Thoughts, fascinations! a pure speck, a dash

of God in every soul? crossing the rifts
of ancient separation – darkling drifts
in the universe's minute-old quark-slush.

4. Fool
A later time; a landscape with no name,
nor picturable: – six miles down, paper-flat,
the stranger fish slide out of the mind's sight –
no, that's not it –: the constructs of a dream,

blocks of no-word, no-images' deep form:
fine-tuned – even the lightest touch of thought
– as act of measurement the quantum-state –
rethrows the fitful web, the exquisite frame.

As this: in a pine-wood sitting (long back),
a little cool fell, and the edge-ferns stirred:
I sensed – outside sense – the massless dead,

massed, in other than Time; un-nerved, unmeshed.
Or, oddment comforts; – one moon-hidden walk,
the heart, obscurely, probed: – fields, silver-lashed.

5.
A certain slant of light over the look-out,
a play of eye, air-clusters reassessed –
and the spare under-etching is outpressed,
few, perfect strokes, the stylussed distillate.

'A little thing, the size of a hazel nut,
all that is made': structure of nothing – almost –
shot through with mind the star-ash, streaming dusts –
the indivisible veers to spirit.

Other shapes of reality: Padre Pio,
with his old palms blood-oozing; the tumour,
touched, of the atheist investigator,

shrinking, drying away: – the scarab-dream
of the rationalist; the thing dinned into the room,
gold! freeing her from spacetime's nowhere-arrow.

6.
This self-conscious creation, this strange Word;
these crawled-to-land-lubbers, a tender race –
awkward of heart, in our drawn-uprightness;
rearing ourselves as we go – soared, seared, strayed:

and this, a puzzle – the long patience of God,
the self-shrinking, the chosen powerlessness;
does he touch, ponder the soul's carapace,
creep these bleak heaths, pick up trace warmths, long-buried?

We grow as we will, and as we have gathered:
each buzz across synapse lays down a mote –
and crusts our children's children, even as we

were, are, built on. By axe-resistant knot
and lump, he waits; by his own laws tethered –
this aeons-grown, this free complexity!

7. Cell
I was running; running with the ball at last! –
had caught (I thought) Unknowing; through Reason
had pressed, slashed, as through a thicket of thorn.
I dreamed, now, of a lonely vale stone-dressed,

high-called with birds, their trailing airs criss-crossed:
I – soaked with mist, windblown – would from some cairn
ride the outspeeding edge, the van-electrons –
intimate, each, with God – all told, all paced.

'Know this, first,' said the old desert Fathers,
'God is unreachable – but that's no matter:
say the prayers – expect no phenomena,

no dropping blood, no Christ-stream in the aethers:
a life, with its routines – food, fuel, water,
prayer-grind – the constant check, pull, of the tuner.'

8.
A jump of time: here, here, cloistered in cell
I am; a transplant, newish, taking root –
but I have not – not yet – engaged with, caught
these sliding alien earths, this prayer-soil.

How slow I am, how slow! a clumsy toil,
a disentangling – jumping jacks of thought –:
the pressing world, its unloved urgent might –
and prayer, what feather-strokes, attritions frail?

Old Gordian knots arise – as when a child
I'd lie, the room receding, before sleep,
and nameless tasks appeared – burdens twelve deep

to balance on a pin; massed tangles, wild
dense briar, or such, across some vital road –
chunks of mind-drift, beyond the borders of word.

9.
Some settling; setting up of a routine:
thought-shapes are building; partial patterns of prayer
part-form – puzzle of pieces on the floor!
as heart-shrunken Kay, cold to the bone,

in walls of ancient ice, with clinking plane
and sliver laboured: tearless cipherer.
– We are all riddlers; would tease out the Sufferer –
shards of nothing we turn, throw, and spin.

I thought myself of Cana's lashings of grape –
the wine-soaked stone, the dripping jar-lip,
a wedding to remember: he was grave

(as I imagined) – lone; austerely watched.
The atoms of him lap against the curve
of time, and stuff; my old stern God, thin-stretched.

10. Night
I was a player always: walked with straws
– no, not that real – people of the wish,
in cities changeable as clouds – mish-mash
of wraith! That was well, as a child – some days

I'd *see* my shock-haired Peter John – he stares,
even now, dinting the grass, that elfin-flesh,
that fairy gold of goblin, strange fish.
– But I hung back – who knows why? – with shadows.

– And now, they are become ghosts of the lie:
my windows, smeared with a tough tarnish.
But I would walk – I fear – a harsh plain,

without chimaeras, *ignes fatui*.
Well, say the saints, we scrape, scrape; and yearn –
part for old purities, part for old ash.

11.
I have lived by the pictures in others' eyes
– mostly: who is this sketch, this gleam of bone,
pale indication, paint-by-numbers man?
A brittle bunch of stalks – King Tut's flowers,

the sharp air-rush upon tomb-centuries,
the fall to dust! – I am stripped lonely down –
my half-dreamed, chattering path, my story, broken:
how bleak, austere, the way of hiddenness!

I am wrenched round – to what reality? –
over and over: the frost-fields of theory: –
to fierce-cold space; infinity of apes

and typewriters – each one eternally taps,
and Hamlet roams the rotten state, joker –
chance precision of the blind Watchmaker.

12.
Are we – few – of all most to be pitied,
plying our prayers to mindless geometries,
in echoed chantries singing to rottedness?
– I'd known of doubts: imagined, half-elated,

a kind of beauty of the unfruited
aching light-years – the cooling whirling whizz
flying outwards, its own tale. – But these days
I am damped down; idleness, clotted.

Does God exist? – from this stifled place,
who cares? It is not dark – no obscure Tower,
no stern Childe, seeking: just a stasis of air –

a scum of molecules, a glueyness.
Sit out the thicks of time: we souls, gelid –
chips of adamant, scatter of buds, dead.

Part Two

13. World
When I was young I backpacked in the East
– Europe, that is – over the lakes of ice,
with their still weeds, suspended fishiness:
beneath the airless pack, the crystal waste,

all slowed, slowed – or dead. And the dead roost
in every grove, about the burial place –
where are they not? relentlessly, they press
into each skin, bread, brick; exigeant dust.

God was put on trial in one of the camps,
found guilty – the Heavens empty – still, they prayed.
The drag of us – we swing away from God,

deep-ripped with our own weight; the threads of mind
that twist, tightly, with ours: that infant hand
we saw, bar-twined, rattling over the ramps.

14.
I'd visited the Wolf's Rampart – bent block
and concrete buckle; its stern name his pride.
What should we call it? bunker of the dead,
of withered souls: by paths, the silver bark

of rustled ice-twig – old enough – snow-shake
in dark folds settling; black soak, where they trod.
Weight of their works! – ice, soil, blizzarded
into the high deep cuttings; set like rock.

The found prayer, wrapped about the baby's arm,
forgiving all; intercession offered –
a lever made of matchwood, fly-foot nudge?

The trains still roll by, over ridge on ridge
of iron snow. – My child's Deus, grim –
did he kick-start Creation, stand aside?

15.
Dislocated, roaring humanity! –
wrenched out of kilter, hobbled foot to wrist –
roaring, eating the gravel where he'd paced:
what Shadow-Kong from old-scooped cavity,

what plague from our deep soil, wracked and knotty?
They hated, planned, by six-foot-thick walls, lost –
spinning off cordless, treading on black space.
– Those eerie granite crumps, the frostbirch beauty!

Bone, muscle, water, gristle globes of eye,
parcels of nerves shunted over the plains –
heaped stuffs: details, trial bundles in vans –

monstrous; and yet – their mass slides over me
even now – the terror-tangle, goaded on:
– but the yerk out of the dark, its hideous pain!

16. Root
– The Jew, Jesus, the wandering Nazarene
(the Gospel joke – 'Can any good thing come
from Nazareth?'): he carried the banked loam
of pasts, like all of us; the mad son,

pacing and sweating in the Death Row garden,
alien, impaled on this I Am:
God, crawled into the little shell of time,
nailed to an armature of brain, and bone.

A derelict; a shouter in the street,
evangelist of nothing; poor, crackfoot:
all this had always been – the steady state,

the thrown-off fizz of us in press of gas.
He gave the lie – creation's hole at heart:
could God not know? a fool, and powerless?

17.
Dead, stiffening; a settling of the blood,
old crabs of hands: and then the slow quaver,
minute shocks – jolts of atom – crackling over;
a turning of earth, breaking of dense clod –

this suffering matter locked to death, untied:
and he treks universes, Christ the mover –
bolas of molecules, electron-rover,
shepherd of the galaxies' outspeed.

That cry, a dying lie? – arms forced open,
he pressed into his strange bitter creation:
zooms round the vast palaces of the bread,

that passionate fission/fusion, this God-man:
undergirder, roosting there with the dead –
palming the little nut; printer, imprinted.

18.
Those microscopic sea-tossed chains of us –
breathers; cold, innocent, and still at one:
slow shoot of soul; push, wrench, of cell; we yearn,
and tear away – pack the long bleeds in ice.

Prayer; that shuffle of air, the butterflies
there – there – tipping a scale beyond precision,
and who knows what far winds, what waters risen?
what shift in the dispersed blood's ardent course?

– It was Spring, at the camps; a haze of flowers
over the Polish plain, the ghost barracks:
beyond, jade patches – a rich bonemeal grass.

Cored with a mote of ice, still the heart seeks –
the Christ-dust swirls, settles, underlocks; –
the quiet, the green of sward, where the ash is.

Notes to 'The Solitary'

3. line 8: ref. *Ezekiel* 37
5. lines 5-6: from *Revelations of Divine Love* by Dame Julian of Norwich
9. lines 9-11: ref. *John* 2:1-11
12. line 1: ref. *1 Cor.* 15: 17-19
13. line 12: ref. St. Augustine, *Confessions*, Book V11, 17
14. line 1: Wilczy Szaniec (translated Wolf's Rampart or Wolf's Lair) is Hitler's bunker in N.E. Poland
16. lines 2-3: ref. *John* 1.46
    line 4: ref. *Mark* 3.21
    line 13: ref. *Mark* 15.34 and *Matthew* 27.46

Acknowledgements

Acknowledgements are due to the editors of the following publications where some of these poems first appeared: *Poetry Salzburg Review, Poetry Wales, Poetry Review, Leviathon Quarterly, Borderlines.*

Also thanks to the Hawthornden Fellowship: this collection was partly written at Hawthorden Castle.

Also by Vuyelwa Carlin

Marble Sky

How We Dream of the Dead

"An impressive collectiopn, to which one can come back
repeatedly and still be surprised." – *Orbis*

Midas' Daughter

"Poem for poem, Midas' Daughter is a stunning book,
the work of a voluptuarist, wordsmith, hex,
the best first collection for years."
– *Michael Hulse, Acumen*